GREEN CRAFTS

# Cool Crafts
with
# Seeds, Beans, and Cones

by Jen Jones

green projects for Resourceful Kids

CAPSTONE PRESS
a capstone imprint

Snap Books are published by Capstone Press,
151 Good Counsel Drive, P.O. Box 669, Mankato, Minnesota 56002.
www.capstonepub.com

Books published by Capstone Press are manufactured with paper
containing at least 10 percent post-consumer waste.

*Library of Congress Cataloging-in-Publication Data*
Jones, Jen.
  Cool crafts with seeds, beans, and cones : green projects for resourceful kids / by Jen Jones.
    p. cm.—(Snap books. Green crafts)
  Summary: "Step-by-step instructions for crafts made from seeds, beans, and cones and information about reusing and
recycling"—Provided by publisher.
  Includes bibliographical references and index.
  ISBN 978-1-4296-4767-0 (library binding)
  1.  Nature craft—Juvenile literature. 2.  Seeds in art—Juvenile literature. 3.  Recycling (Waste, etc.)—Juvenile literature.  I.
Title.
  TT157.J646 2011
  745.5—dc22
                        2010027904

**Editorial Credits**
Lori Shores, editor; Gene Bentdahl, designer; Sarah Schuette, photo stylist;
    Marcy Morin, project production; Laura Manthe, production specialist

**Photo Credits**
All photos by Capstone Studio/Karon Dubke except:
Jen Jones, 32
Shutterstock/Amy Johansson (chain link fence); Ian O'Hanlon (recycling stamp)

Essential content terms are **bold** and are defined at the bottom of the page
where they first appear.

Printed in the United States of America in North Mankato, Minnesota.
092010
005933CGS11

# Table of Contents

**6**

**8**

**14**

**18**

**24**

**26**

# Introduction

Saving the Earth can seem overwhelming. But reusing materials to make crafts is a small step that can make a big difference. Give new life to beans, seeds, and cones, and plant the seeds for a greener planet at the same time! After all, even little steps—and crafts—add up to one big change for the planet.

Simple items from your backyard or pantry are all you need for these cool crafts. Make a dazzling night-light or an eye-catching vase. Or get sudsy with some homemade soap. Whatever you choose, get ready to have some fun. After all, making **eco-friendly** art isn't just good for the planet—it's also a good time!

**eco-friendly**—marked by or showing concern for the environment

## Go Metric!

It's easy to change measurements to metric! Just use this chart.

| To change | into | multiply by |
|---|---|---|
| inches | centimeters | 2.54 |
| inches | millimeters | 25.4 |
| feet | meters | .305 |
| yards | meters | .914 |

## Did You Know?

- Pinecones can be either male or female. Male pinecones are much smaller than female pinecones.

- Seeds have an amazing sense of direction. They're geotropic, which means that even if planted upside down, they'll still grow upward.

- Beans come in more than 13,000 varieties around the world.

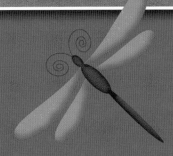

# Picture This

Think outside the box and use beans instead of paint for your next masterpiece. Beans come in a wide variety of colors, shapes, and sizes. Using them to make a **mosaic** is a great way to show them off. Anything from soup beans to kidney beans to black beans will do. By mixing colorful beans and creativity, the results are cool as can be!

## Here's what you need:
- hole puncher
- clear plastic lid, round, at least 6 inches wide
- pencil
- white paper
- dried beans, assorted colors
- craft glue
- small paintbrush
- ½-inch to ¾-inch wide ribbon, about 1 foot long

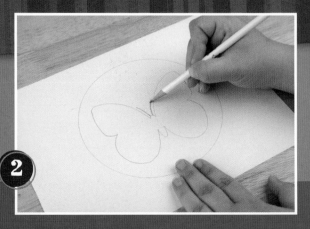

## Step 1
Punch two holes through a clear plastic lid as if at 11 and 1 on a clock. Avoid gluing beans over these holes in steps 4 and 5.

## Step 2
Trace the lid on white paper. In the circle, draw a simple design or image to use as the guide for your mosaic.

## Step 3
Place the drawing under the plastic lid. Select a section of the picture that will be all the same color. Pick out the beans you want to use for this section.

## Step 4
Using the drawing as a guide, apply glue onto the lid over the chosen section with a small paintbrush.

## Step 5
Press the beans onto the glue. Be sure to place the beans close together so the plastic doesn't show through.

## Step 6 *(not pictured)*
Continue applying glue and adding beans section by section until the entire picture is filled in. Let dry for one week.

## Step 7
Thread ribbon through the holes in the lid. Tie ribbon at the top for hanging.

*Tip:* Stumped for what to draw? Flip through your favorite magazine for some ideas.

**mosaic**—a picture or pattern made from small, colored shapes

# Good Clean Fun

Go from duds to suds by making your own soap at home. Poppy seeds give this soap texture to help soften your skin. And the added **essential oil** will have you smelling lemon-fresh. Get ready to pamper yourself!

## Here's what you need:
- melt-and-pour glycerin soap base, 14 ounces
- large glass liquid measuring cup
- plastic spoon
- measuring spoons
- 1 tablespoon lemon essential oil
- yellow liquid soap dye
- 1 tablespoon poppy seeds
- petroleum jelly
- plastic ice cube tray
- toothpick
- rubbing alcohol
- small spray bottle
- plastic wrap

## Step 1
Place soap base in a large glass liquid measuring cup. Heat in microwave for 30 seconds at a time, stirring occasionally, until soap is completely melted.

## Step 2
Add 1 tablespoon lemon essential oil to the soap and stir.

## Step 3
Add 20 drops of yellow liquid soap dye. Stir until the color is even throughout.

## Step 4
Keep stirring until melted mixture is thick like pudding but still pourable. Add poppy seeds and stir to distribute seeds evenly.

*Tip:* Glycerine, essential oils, and soap dye can all be found at craft stores.

**essential oil**—oil from a plant that is used to make perfumes or flavors

To finish this project, turn to the next page. ⇨

### Step 5
Use your fingers to spread a thin layer of petroleum jelly inside the spaces of a plastic ice cube tray.

### Step 6
Carefully pour the soap into the ice cube tray. Stir each cube with a toothpick as it sets so the poppy seeds don't settle at the bottom.

### Step 7
Lightly mist rubbing alcohol on top of the soap with a small spray bottle. The rubbing alcohol will keep bubbles from forming on the surface.

**Step 8** *(not pictured)*
Put the tray on a counter or other safe place where it won't be disturbed. Allow soap to dry for two days.

**Step 9**
Place the ice cube tray in the freezer for five minutes. Pop the soaps from the tray as you would ice cubes.

**Step 10**
Wrap soap cubes separately in plastic wrap for storing.

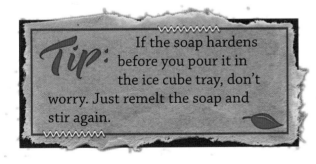

*Tip:* If the soap hardens before you pour it in the ice cube tray, don't worry. Just remelt the soap and stir again.

# Fresh and Bright

Pinecones don't just smell pretty—they look pretty too! Show them off in this sweet-smelling night-light. This craft lets you capture that great outdoors smell in your home all year long.

## Here's what you need:
- ½ cup water
- spray bottle
- pine essential oil
- small pinecones, about 60
- plastic zipper-seal bag, gallon size
- twinkle lights, strand of 50 lights
- clear tape
- clear glass jar, 4-quart size

## Step 1
Put water into a spray bottle. Add seven drops of essential oil.

## Step 2
Place pinecones in the sink and spray them with the water and oil. Seal the pinecones in a plastic bag and let sit for 24 hours.

## Step 3
Plug in the string of lights. Leaving enough cord to reach the outlet, tape the light string to the outside of a clear glass jar near the bottom.

## Step 4
Run the string of lights up to the top of the jar. Tape the cord between the lights in a few places so that the cord stays attached to the jar.

## Step 5
Using the other end of the light string, make a circle around the inside bottom of the jar.

## Step 6
Add a layer of pinecones into the jar. Then make another circle with the lights.

## Step 7 *(not pictured)*
Repeat steps 5 and 6 until the jar is full.

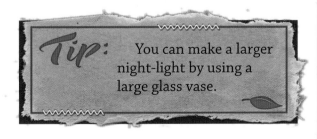

Tip: You can make a larger night-light by using a large glass vase.

# Gorgeous Gifts

When you get a gift, it's tempting to quickly tear open the box. Yet with these great gift boxes, your friends may just stare at the lovely designs you've created. They'll barely be able to contain themselves after receiving one of these cute containers!

**Here's what you need:**
- small cardboard box with lid
- newspaper
- acrylic paint, any color
- 2 small paintbrushes
- white colored pencil
- tacky glue
- seeds and beans in a variety of colors
- 1 tablespoon water
- small bowl

## Step 1

Place a small cardboard box and lid on newspaper. Paint the entire outside of the box and lid. Let dry.

## Step 2

Place the lid on the box. Use a white colored pencil to trace a line around the box at the bottom edge of the lid.

## Step 3

Lightly draw out simple patterns, such as stripes or triangles, on each side of the box and lid. Avoid the top edge of the box that will be covered by the lid.

## Step 4

Use a clean paintbrush to apply a thick layer of tacky glue to one section of a design on the box.

## Step 5

Press your choice of beans or seeds over the glue. Try to place the seeds or beans close together so the box doesn't show through.

## Step 6 *(not pictured)*

Working on one section at a time, repeat steps 4 and 5 until the entire box and lid are covered.

## Step 7

Mix 1 tablespoon glue and 1 tablespoon water in a small bowl. Use the paintbrush to apply glue mixture over entire box and lid. Allow to dry overnight.

**Tip:** For a more casual look, mix the beans and seeds together on a plate. Cover one surface of the box or lid in glue and press into the seeds. Repeat with all sides of the box and lid.

# Here Birdy, Birdy!

If you think you know all there is to know about pinecone bird feeders, think again. Load up this pinecone garland with peanut butter and bird snacks and—voila! Dinner for birds is served. No doubt, all the birds will be flocking to your yard!

## Here's what you need:
- wire snips
- floral wire, about 8 feet
- ruler
- 12 pinecones, various types and sizes
- **jute** twine, about 3½ feet
- newspaper
- spoon
- 1 cup smooth peanut butter
- 1 cup birdseed
- ½ cup raisins, soaked in water to soften

1

2

3

## Step 1
Have an adult use wire snips to cut floral wire into 12 8-inch pieces.

## Step 2
Wrap one wire around a pinecone at the base, tucking the wire inside the pinecone's scales. Twist the ends of the wire together leaving a long tail. Repeat with all pinecones.

## Step 3
Lay a piece of **jute** on a table or counter covered in newspaper. Arrange the wired pinecones along the sides of the jute, alternating large and small pinecones. Leave about 10 inches of jute on one end without pinecones.

## Step 4
Attach pinecones to the jute by tightly winding the wire tails around the jute. Twist the wire back on itself to secure. Tuck in the end so no sharp points are left.

## Step 5
Use a spoon to spread peanut butter on the pinecones, covering the top of each scale.

## Step 6
Sprinkle birdseed over the pinecones. Press raisins onto some of the scales. Let sit for 24 hours to harden.

## Step 7
Hang the bird feeder from a tree by tying the end of the jute without pinecones around a branch.

> **Tip:** Try adding cracked corn, sunflower seeds, and berries to the pinecones. Some birds even enjoy a treat of grape or strawberry jelly.

**jute**—a strong plant fiber that is woven to make rope and coarse material

# Jack-o'- Jewelry

Not only are pumpkin seeds tasty, they're also très chic! You can turn pumpkin seeds into jewelry in a few simple steps. Once you make this fun necklace, try your hand at a bracelet. Then you'll have a set to add to your **accessory** collection.

## Here's what you need:
- 2 cups pumpkin seeds, cleaned and roasted
- cardboard
- spray paint, any color(s)
- scissors
- clear elastic string, about 2 feet
- large sewing needle
- thick cardboard

### How to Roast Pumpkin Seeds:
Rinse seeds in a strainer and pat dry with a towel. Place seeds in a single layer on a baking sheet. Have an adult help you bake the seeds in the oven at 350 degrees Fahrenheit for 30 minutes. Stir the seeds every 10 minutes while baking.

1

## Step 1
Lay pumpkin seeds in a single layer on cardboard. Spray paint both sides of the pumpkin seeds following directions on can. Let dry.

## Step 2
Cut a piece of clear elastic string about 2 feet long. Slide the string through the eye of a large sewing needle. Tie a knot in one end of the string.

## Step 3
Lay a seed flat on top of a thick piece of cardboard. Poke the needle through the middle of the seed to the cardboard.

## Step 4
Pull the needle through, and slide the seed to the knot at the end.

## Step 5 *(not pictured)*
Repeat steps 3 and 4 until you've strung enough seeds to fit around your neck.

## Step 6
Tie both ends of the elastic string into a secure knot.

**Tip:** To add some dazzle to your necklace, place a fancy bead between each seed.

**accessory**—something, such as a belt or jewelry, that goes with your clothes

# Handy Holder

Give yourself a hand—for real! This adorable hand-shaped jewelry holder comes in handy on any gal's dresser. Rescue your favorite accessories from that dark jewelry box and display them as works of art. Hang bracelets from the thumb, and stack your favorite rings on the fingers. You can even punch small holes in the palm to display earrings.

X X X X

## Here's what you need:
- pencil
- **thick cardboard**
- **ruler**
- **scissors**
- **craft glue**
- **craft paint**
- **paintbrush**
- **fabric square, at least 9 inches wide by 9 inches long**
- **white chalk**
- **ribbon, ¼-inch wide, about 3 feet**
- **dried beans, about 1 to 2 cups**

X X X X

## Step 1

Trace one of your hands and wrist onto a piece of thick cardboard. At the bottom of the wrist, draw a 4- by 1-inch rectangle.

## Step 2

Use scissors to cut out the tracing. Trace this hand cutout onto another section of cardboard and cut out.

## Step 3

Glue the two hand pieces together to make one thick hand. Do not glue the rectangles together.

## Step 4

Use paint to decorate the hand. Decorate one side at a time, allowing it to dry before turning over to decorate other side.

## Step 5

Measure and cut a 9-inch square from a piece of fabric. Trim the corners of the fabric to make a circle.

To finish this project, turn to the next page. ⇨

### Step 6
Use white chalk to make 27 marks about 1 inch apart along the edge of the circle. Snip tiny holes at each mark by pinching the fabric and making a small cut on the fold.

### Step 7
Hold fabric so the printed or colorful side faces away from you. Insert ribbon through one hole from the side facing you to the colorful side. Weave the ribbon through all of the holes as if sewing, going in front and behind the fabric.

### Step 8
Pull the ends of the ribbon to form a loose bowl shape with the fabric.

## Step 9

Set the fabric bowl flat on your workspace. Pour about one-third of the beans into the bowl. Insert the holder into the beans so the hand is sticking straight up. Bend the rectangles so they flare out to the front and back with beans underneath. Pour in the rest of the beans.

## Step 10

Pull the ribbon tight so the fabric bunches up around the beans and hand. Tie the ribbon in a bow.

**Tip:** To make the hand more stable, add a bit of glue around the inside rim of the fabric. Press to the hand and let dry.

# Mirror, Mirror

Mirror, mirror on the wall—who's the most eco-friendly of all? With this pinecone-framed mirror, you'll be able to primp and preen to your heart's content. Consider the project a reflection of your dedication to saving the Earth!

## Here's what you need:
- **small and medium pinecones, about 40**
- **newspaper**
- **clear sealer spray**
- **8- by 10-inch picture frame, wood**
- **glue gun and hot glue**
- **8- by 10-inch mirror, ¾ inch thick**

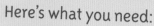

**1**

**2**

## Step 1

Set pinecones on newspaper. Spray each pinecone with clear sealer following the instructions on the can. Make sure to cover both the inside and outside of each pinecone. Let dry for 15 minutes.

## Step 2

Remove backing and glass from picture frame. Set the backing aside for step 6. The glass can be recycled or saved for another craft project.

## Step 3

Hot glue one pinecone to the front of the frame at the top left corner. The pinecone should be positioned so the flat bottom is against the frame.

## Step 4

Hot glue another pinecone to the frame. Position this one on its side. It should be at an angle so it is as close as possible to the first pinecone.

## Step 5

Continue adding pinecones around the frame, arranging them standing up or on their sides to cover the frame. Let dry for one hour.

## Step 6

Place mirror into the frame and reattach the backing.

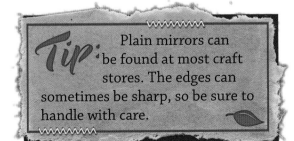

**Tip:** Plain mirrors can be found at most craft stores. The edges can sometimes be sharp, so be sure to handle with care.

# Bottle It Up

Regular vases are oh-so-yesterday. Transform a boring bottle into a stylish vase bursting with floral finesse. By using colorful beans and a pattern of your choosing, you'll have a one-of-a-kind vase. Add colorful daisies or sassy sunflowers to truly brighten your space.

**Here's what you need:**
- measuring cup with pour spout
- dried beans, various colors and sizes
- clear glass beverage bottle with wide mouth, clean and label removed
- fake flowers
- ribbon, ½-inch wide

**1**

**2**

## Step 1
Use a measuring cup to pour a layer of beans about 1 inch deep into a glass bottle. Tap the bottom of the bottle on a table to pack the beans in tightly.

## Step 2
Add another layer of beans using a different kind of bean. Smaller or larger layers will create different-sized stripes.

## Step 3
Continue adding layers of beans and tapping the bottom until the bottle is full.

## Step 4
Arrange fake flowers in the vase by poking them into the beans.

## Step 5
Tie a ribbon around the neck of the bottle.

**Tip:** You can also add glitter or sand in with the beans to spice up the look.

# Green Crafting Facts

🐞 Since ancient times, people have used natural products to beautify their skin. Today you can hit the pantry to see what nature has to offer. Try mixing ¼ cup each of honey and flax seed for a rich facial scrub. Leave on for 10 minutes, and don't forget to thank Mother Nature!

🐞 Want another great way to use seeds to help the environment? Consider writing letters and invitations on seed paper. After it's read, this paper can be buried in the garden and grown into wildflowers. Talk about recycling at its finest!

🐞 If you love to watch birds, plant some sunflowers in your yard. A sunflower makes a beautiful, all-natural bird feeder. Plant sunflowers in full sun where you can see them through a window or from the patio. It won't be long before some feathered friends stop by.

When it comes to crafting with cones, you have plenty of options once you start looking. Although we usually say "pinecones," pine trees are only one kind of tree that produces seed cones. **Conifer** trees all over the world produce many different cones.

**conifer**—a tree with needles and cones that keeps its needles all year

# Glossary

**accessory** (ak-SEH-suh-ree)—something, such as a belt or jewelry, that goes with your clothes

**conifer** (KOHN-uh-fuhr)—a tree with needles and cones that keeps its needles all year

**eco-friendly** (EE-koh-frend-lee)—inflicting minimal or no harm to the environment; eco-friendly is short for ecologically friendly

**environment** (in-VY-ruhn-muhnt)—the natural world of the land, water, and air

**essential oil** (i-SEN-shuhl OIL)—oil from a plant that is used to make perfumes or flavors

**jute** (JOOT)—a strong plant fiber that is woven to make rope and coarse material

**mosaic** (moh-ZAY-ik)—pictures or patterns made from small, colored shapes

**très chic** (TRAY SHEEK)—very stylish or fashionable

# Read More

**Anton, Carrie.** *Earth Smart Crafts: Transform Toss-Away Items into Fun Accessories, Gifts, Room Décor, and More!* Middleton, Wis.: American Girl, 2009.

**Jones, Jen.** *Cool Crafts with Flowers, Leaves, and Twigs: Green Projects for Resourceful Kids.* Green Crafts. Mankato, Minn.: Capstone Press, 2011.

**Monaghan, Kimberly.** *Organic Crafts: 75 Earth-Friendly Art Activities.* Chicago: Chicago Review Press, 2007.

RECYCLE

# Internet Sites

FactHound offers a safe, fun way to find Internet sites related to this book. All of the sites on FactHound have been researched by our staff.

Here's all you do:

Visit *www.facthound.com*

Type in this code: **9781429647670**

**Super-cool stuff!** Check out projects, games and lots more at
**www.capstonekids.com**

## About the Author

A Midwesterner-turned-California girl, Jen Jones loves to be in nature and is proud to be part of any project that makes our world a greener place! Jen is a Los Angeles-based writer who has authored more than 35 books for Capstone Press. Her stories have been published in magazines such as *American Cheerleader, Dance Spirit, Ohio Today,* and *Pilates Style.* She has also written for E! Online, MSN, and PBS Kids, as well as being a Web site producer for major talk shows such as *The Jenny Jones Show, The Sharon Osbourne Show,* and *The Larry Elder Show.* Jen is a member of the Society of Children's Book Writers and Illustrators.